Ndewo, Colorado

poems by

Uche Ogbuji

Aldrich Press

ISBN13:978-0615886084

Cover photograph: Uche Ogbuji

Aldrich Press
24600 Mountain Avenue, 35
Hemet, California 92544

Dear Sam
Gratias tibi ago magnas!

Ndewo, Colorado

For Lori, with whom I've settled this land.

Acknowledgments

First publication credits for poems included in this manuscript:

"Endo," (from "Mountain Tanka") January 2012,
  Mountain Gazette
"Fever Pitch Tent," 1996, *ELF: Eclectic Literary Forum*
"Mountain Summer," 1996, *ELF: Eclectic Literary Forum*
"July 4th at Arapahoe Basin," 2012, *Colorado Poet's Center*
"Colorado…Du Grand Soleil…Du Vent," May 2013, *String Poet*
"El Cabeceo de Niwot," 2012, *Colorado Poet's Center*
"Autumn Equinox Creature Song," June 2013, *Qarrtsiluni*
"Catamount," June 2013, *Leveler*
"Above Left Hand Canyon," March 2013, *IthacaLit*
"Rag Tags," (from "Janus") October 2012, *Red Fez Magazine*
"Transit of Venus, Fiske Planetarium, Boulder Colorado,"
  June, 2012, *The Nervous breakdown*

I also thank Wendy Chin-Tanner and my other constant companions in poetry and editing. I thank Cynthia K Erbes, editor of the once and ever superb *ELF: Eclectic Literary Forum,* the first editor who reassured me that I had not migrated from Nigeria to the U.S. to find myself entirely alone in my understanding of poetry. I thank Erika Rae who nudged me toward finding my pen peers online. I thank David Mason and Wendy Videlock who have with constant kindness integrated me into the accomplished yet warm community of poets in Colorado, and who have taught me much about how to write from this extraordinary place.

Oh, men of Colorado save the tree!
And build in our own state its glory strong,
Here let it sing the message sweet and free,
'Tis sweeter far than any poet's song.

—from "The Message of the Tree" (Denver Times, 1921)
by Alice Polk Hill, First Poet Laureate of Colorado, 1919-1921

Table of Contents

Mountain Tanka

Earned Turns

Breaths in grateful gasps
Mark my pilgrimage upslope;
Weight of equipment,
Weight of anticipation:
Up next the gold hill down-rush.

Endo

Head upside home fried
Champagne powder, I lip-smack
Fatback and ignore
Scores of dive judges above
Grinning from slack chair front row.

Nighty Alpine

What a pop-rock stream,
This ribbon of Milky Way
That bites swirly white
Into vacuum-cold lungs, knifes
Exposure on my mind's film.

Fever Pitch Tent

The howling wind nearly carried us
Over the stubborn campfire
With twigs caught in its bustle and fuss,
Whisked though sere mangrove,
Twisted, dry roots and coarse briar,
To shrub grass coating the hills above.

Animals, living and dead, pressing
Against our tent, kicked the careless
Hotchpot of bags and bottles dressing
The illegal ash pit, and danced their derision:
Not scampering game in our headlights, but fearless
Totems from roaming id. So, lying as in mass prison,

Huddled together as we were,
Each chest against the other,
Linking the fire of clear
Youth, we defied exposure of dreamless
Heads in a noisy veil. Unable to smother
The fire outside, we knit into seamless

Bulwark the rutted rock
On which we lay. Having fought
And laughed, hungered and sung, having gawked
At slopes and swifts that clutch
Life at its stitch to taut
Flesh membranes, we knew the coming touch

Of dawn would break the storm into dewdrops
On earth, whose pores, cleansed by mist,
Would reabsorb these ancient highland spirits.
Knowing our skin would save us all, we slept.

Colorado...Du Grand Soleil...Du Vent

Continental divide is slingshot cord,
Flyover country's catapult of storms;
The wind has plains to sweep and streams to ford
And hills to shape into outrageous forms.
Front Range spreads unexpected *cococure*,
Three hundred sun-blessed days of luxury,
She feels our gratitude, but to be sure
She sends the sometime winds for augury.
Broken trees and ranging tumbleweeds,
Clack of gates and loosened roofing tiles,
Flash floods, cyclones, coronal radar blips,
And locust swarm of wicked thistle seeds.
Thus nature with these micro-metered trials
Hints at our peril of apocalypse.

Wayfaring Mysteries

I ran and the absence beside me rose up,
Stilt man of history's long shade, where bison
Specialists stepped over the plains lightly,
Where passenger cars lit upon Denver's
Union station. I'm alone, but I count
And somehow keep coming up infinity
As Emmaus of the red rock draws near
This bounding mystery, what is it to me?

I'm parched...but lo! Well watered! Whose sudden hand
Materialized this miracle canteen?
It's semi-arid yet all this greenery
Mocks my senses like a cartoon mirage,
While from the garden's hidden, central fount
Al Kizr sings the edge of what I see:
"There's so much mercy in what first seems harsh..."
This bounding mystery, what is it to me?

I ran and an absence beside me hinted
At it's form while guiding me through treacherous
Rock byways; Great Krishna's guarantee
Drove forth the chariot of my explorations
And proved that all the glories shown in light
Were but a jot in the vision of my *chi*,
These bush-of-ghost companions who crowd in
This bounding mystery, who are they to me?

Note: Chi—Igbo concept of the self-spirit, similar in idea to the soul

Mountain Summer

The woman and child in bathing suits
Trudge, plough, step high over dunes,
Crunch ice for footing, in measured stride.
Turning about, they leap on the saucer and fly
Merrily down pitted slopes into raptures,
Finding their break against banking snow…

Mountain winter defies the order,
Denies the bonding of elements.
Wooded snow and falling wind
Force repentance through birdsong.
Unwaning sun razes gooseflesh,
Floods snow, and drowns the senses,
Pitched in broken bottle rainbow battle
With trenchant ice-cold mountain streams.

Turning about, they fly to the patronage
Of local rebel ethers.
Settling into the mountain's lap
They bask in untimely solstice.
Measuring with our watches,
We shun the whim of Mother Earth.
Shattering sense to our goggling eyes,
She reminds us of her stubborn clout.

July 4th at Arapahoe Basin

Massifs of the divide cut into delicate
Sky with their gnomic, craggy brown.
Settled deep into Colorado's legend
I look out from this million-year-old crown.

The wizened dignity of ice patch streaks
Ignores the upstart clouds of matching white.
Settled deep into Colorado's legend
What mythic zero summer at this height!

The titan expanse below is tempered
By tall thickets of scrabbling, hard won green.
Settled deep into Colorado's legend
What is the magic engine of this scene?

Hardy terrain well symbolized by scree
Baring its loose-tooth shards of angled grey.
Settled deep into Colorado's legend
What mountain *gris-gris* ghosted me away?

The noon angle of high infinity
Dons a body of hot flame, unfiltered blue.
Settled deep into Colorado's legend
Set in the god-aged fastness of this view.

Descent

Pishsh!
The *pishsh*
Snow flies *pishsh*
Head height, foot flung,
Cold in crouching shock
As mouths Oh! into smiles
Where brains plot bounds into slush,
Across spray, beating off slow fleece.
Wetness irrupts into propped orbits;
Teardrop jets of extruded mud make paint,
Mark us for tribe as we grasp at each other
Laughing slip-donned wonder as we spin cross-career,
Branch out to secrets aside the sodden thoroughfare.
Pishsh! To the park *pishsh*! panting, cough! *pishsh*!
Kicking off shoes, side-slapping skulls *pishsh*!
To pool yield of gleaming eyes.

We will be back here again, friends as ever,
Where bottom basks topside of fallen sense.

Knowing Snow

Step with a coy crouch
Knowledge fixed within the bed
Shifting weight to float.
What angle of boot attack
Does the slope's repose demand?

Leap springbok memory,
Knowledge fixed within the bed
Back leg snapped upward.
Fleet shadow over snow, bound,
White splash to splash, crust to crust.

Twin-track the postholes
Knowledge fixed within the bed
Friendship's in the gait,
Kissing in foot-sworn echoes,
Love making to spring the thaw.

El Cabeceo de Niwot

Whirl with me in this flatiron shade,
Spin yin-yang teardrops of our hips,
All limbs in strophe and antistrophe:
Firm as pine roots, supple as tulips.

Sway with me to the downslope winds,
Tight to my rope cinched at silk mast
Of your bodice, our spread-sail canvas
Disdaining the stormy forecast.

Trip with me to the tumbleweed turn,
Our steps like seed-bearing branches,
Through restless legging of *corrido*
And strains of Chalino Sánchez.

Vals with me to divide of bedrock,
Springs falling away upon both sides,
Even the moon skips wax on wane
To fortnightly beat about our Ides.

Flow with me along St. Vrain creek,
Mingling with the Poudre and Cherry;
We are the sweet-laden South Platter
Bobbing refreshment to the weary.

Romp with me through this foundling land;
Sing your songs in our common creole—
They're listening, those dancing bears,
Those elks engaged in caracole.

Rachel A. in Colorado, 1995

Same silent crouch for stump as for vista,
You with your camera and object come one,
Midsummer frost returning some equalled admiration
Back along your sight-beam's bold arrow.
Later I can see mountains
Reflected in your clear face
As if you were the film which captured them.

Exclaim Colorado

The apron peaks of home-trim divide
Folded over this black-toppled drainage
Water sets these sun-funked facets leaping
Comes in at the eye this gash-gold spray
Of aspens winking as sky's greys deepen.

The foot-locks of lodgepole green push up
The lighters of the fuse-box chromophyll
Water sets these sun-funked facets leaping
And now descending rank of frost asserts
Its bivouac cap as flag of winter's creeping.

The Summit county microclimate strikes
Its herald note of impending season
What seraph saps the sun-fund in its keeping?
Yet through the sleet-striated air I catch
These fey copses at their stubborn leaping,

Wrapped by signs of soul cyclically setting,
One moon-sault shy of buskined New Year
Water sets these sun-funked facets leaping
Sly pantomime of hemisphere's extreme
When the sun-bairn's supposedly sleeping.

And then O god! The mist-splitting blast
Of Sol direct films the dimmed layers in fire
Water sets these sun-funked facets leaping
Fingers of life's frenzy knead the senses
When this land's wonder germ bursts, ripe for reaping.

On Valerie Haugen's Mount Sopris

And there, pooled like a dream cwm,
Swabbing the skirts of the Mount:
A Sopris spool-out of marshmallow mist,
Strained through the brambles
Into cool, crisp air a quick pinch
Before the vista vertex at the roof;
The brooding thrift of April drip
Moves to excuse itself skyward,
Then down into the grooves that lick
Their way through plains and canyons
To grateful coast; but first, the clouds
Insist, pausing before they doff their tops,
An interlude to slip a soothing
Shift over those who've built hearths
Where they can sip slow comforts
From the generous fingertips
Of highland grooming, alpine grace.

Parachuted

Colorado National Monument, Fruita

It beats attention from our toes
At first, this sparse, grangy gaggle
Of bull rocks verged about the calfs
Who know the urged edge but straggle

Stoic along the perch until fate
Makes good on cracked calamity,
Maturing them in snap-shutter plunge;
They settle, grey salting on scree.

Just as the prankster juniper
Chuckles at her root's sly doing
The ranger's voice snaps me about
From open-mouthed cross-canyon viewing.

"This is Kayenta, foot-loose hold
For roots, and swift life's flash pools."
It seemed the sky dashed rocks down in
Some rage from which it still slow-cools.

Were they storm paratroop assault
Huddling where their brief blanked its lies?
Looking for the native red that
Washed from their fancy of disguise?

No, said ranger, these are slow wave
Reformed in trough of the Triassic;
Long before this REM age they slept
Deeply here, bowstrung, elastic.

How does this land mean me, hurled down
From across Pangea's old never?
Had I no pushy, *sub rosa*
Roots for space and time to sever?

I step assured on brother stone,
Such camp mates with whom I've slumbered;
What juju I spell awakens here,
Those generations unencumbered.

Colorado *Lève Tôt*

It bone-rats the pantry-wall wainscoting
Of shallow dreams, grubbing blitz
At melatonin's spell (flimsy Maginot!)
The white-washed-blue, cloud-bald vista stands off
Silver spider-work of chill-dip moisture
On grateful scrub as I pseudopod my toe
Into this cleansing shock, this gashed reveille,
Ice bath of Colorado *lève tôt*.

Numbness buzzes my tottering column
But fastens at my plantar pressure points
As Styx wicks up my pores in throbbing flow.
I shake loose my dream-caught load, fish-egged
Fitfully on finger-thicket reefs from
White-out dream-ink of kraken love below.
I snatch these wrigglers for my scrap-pad hook—
Ice bath of Colorado *lève tôt*.

Watch the sun at these drastic angles
Burn the fringe of tin-filing-thin needles
And sparse broadleaf in tale's end fireplace glow,
With what seems a mere nod buffering this crack
Of story-court muezzin call as words
Burst their black, silk sac, gems reclaimed from escrow,
Spread on my skin from night-blind plunge into
Ice bath of Colorado *lève tôt*.

First Snow, 2012

Plump and plain this plenitude, harvest *nachspiel*,
Spread on fronds of conifer, filigreed as
Crystal spider-work until morning scythes in,
Feeds on the fruiting.

Nothing emphasizes the needful lung like
Mountain air through over-exposed aurora;
Eyes on true abundance which blankets our brute-sown,
Own sort of excess.

Frost Frieze

This westerly tilt of the sky-glow brim,
Of the red and orange rimmed *chapeau*,
Reveals what earth the heavens floored
To mask its matching, bloody show.

Dawn winches up her curtain cord—
The frieze has spilled to beard the gourd.

The foreign eye diffracts love-light—
Intimate customs seem assault;
When seasons are the countries toured
The tropic serves as violent fault.

Dawn winches up her curtain cord—
The frieze has spilled to beard the gourd.

I'm mapper and mythographer,
The one who moves, but stays a while;
Such mornings sign where I've explored
And mark their place in savage style.

Dawn winches up her curtain cord—
The frieze has spilled to beard the gourd.

Foothills unzip the vista's stays—
Dawn winches up her curtain cord;
Snow smothers autumn's sunrise shades—
The frieze has spilled to beard the gourd.

Denver in Loft and Snow

White flats, white snow flats, fingers
Of grey homes, stubs of grey growth,
Rings of crab-crawl roads, slate rose crosses
Bristling green in garish stands, round white groomed fields,
And ranked beforehand, unruly foot raiding jutting rock,
Nimbus of shallow grey airship-shaped smog,
Towering thatch, blocks in a monolith thicket,
Queerly angled quiver, sheath of stone quills
Acute to front range axis, rods of rule and commerce—
Denver Downtown, boist of plains mounting to dramatic peak;

White plate, prickly grey stands, pallid grey cloud—
A mushroom of life limned on white stock,
Neat box-bound license, each scene set in snow-field speech
    bubbles,
Melt-through rock or metal scrawl, mute tell-tales.

In the foreground uneven Boulder, banks of bosques;
Unnatural black given for green by white glare,
True black on mines, new black on snow-cleared roofs,
My own somewhere along the spur south to Denver,
My own snow suite, ice street, grey walls,
Black roof, brown children, white wife,
Green, white, green heritage,
Black roots, red, white, brown recreation;
Black, white, silvered green life-blood and livelihood.

Below me land of choices, latent longing,
One visit for vista and wonder, next to set roots and tilt polls,
Campaign for clean air, carp against sprawl,
Lawns xeriscaped with donkey, pachyderm or even third way
    pennant
Punch lithe-leisure holes into lumbering ambition and listing loves.

I see the ghost overlay of westing wagons, wandering to claim
    width,
Or tending back towards heartland in retreat from trammelled
    coast,
Or paused and staged in circles, strays in solidarity.

Below me the junction of June junkets, gentle magnet of dreams,
Fulcrum of foreign and familiar, franchise of farm and foundry,
Purple range backbone of bald eagle empire,
Nature-toned nave of adopted nation.

Soon divide itself takes demesnes of the dropping scene:
Watersheds over timber-weed valleys pop view-verged inverts
As if stitched on a blown balloon surface—
White blasts on blue-veined grey-green and black,
All waft to white cloud as we rise and west through winter welkin.

Whistle-white thistledown blown across mottled marine rim of the
    blue vault,
Which sits on the rough crown mountain, master of what distance
suggests as clean calm,
But what local knowledge reveals as a throne under threat,
In the hothouse, harried by pressure from its own subject city.

Janus

Rag Tags

Such rag tags, those clouds!
They're on the sun's dole
All sated at belly
And gleaming at trim.

I've my fill of vagrants
Every way and now up!
Oh bugling rabble,
ski-bum seraphim.

Snowblind

Did you stare yourself an empty house at the orbits?
Worry enough to learn, but be comforted.
Birds will come back again now you're chidden milk white,
Brown and grey flumes giving way eventually to
Rainbow brook below tree line.

New Year's Eve, 2012

I crunch-step through the bank of drift
    In Boulder's ugly shoes
Which buffer frostbite but whose thrift
    Leaves ankles to the news;
I wonder what strange sort of hold
    The Pentateuch inspires
To gospel caroling of cold
    By sullen spirit wires.

I'll have no ashen Wednesday mass
    But *puja* to Ganesh;
The year's dark corpse may load the grass
    But the coming year is fresh.
Talak for grace and fortune
    At the *ajna* chakra point,
Sung to serve life, not importune
    Affirm, not disappoint.

I'm moved against my temper's gauge
    To boot- and wool-coat camp
To cool what's lived in me all age—
    A sacrilegious scamp.
My stiffened fingers still do worry
    Sitar's long choke of frets
My wayward tongue still orders curry
    Of saffron intimates.

And though its chidden face is white,
      This purple majesty,
Though its glories are not recondite
      I praise its mystery.
Its soul black loam with experience
      Leaves restless *atma's* share;
Each new day whistles treasures hence
      When life's lived well aware.

May Day Flakes

Mid Spring Winter comes with sweet insistence.
Falling flake wide like peeling of flayed paint,
Soft like spray of dandelion spore, christens
Groaning grass seedling (plump
Bud florist stock breed), rump
Rock pile from home improvement project feint.

We were supposed to have our fence painted
By this weekend. The letter warned of fines.
That idle council, declaring suburban
Heresy—dire tone
Of grey flanking our home—
Proclaimed our colors well outside the lines.

Tricycles left in front yards, red white-crests,
Play off smooth snow hillocks of soccer balls.
Playground plans, evening sports meets laid to rest,
Schools closed, commutes delayed,
Airport scheduling betrayed,
We stare from windows, stubborn nature's thralls.

The moisture is welcome, our water table,
Plunged to record depths, swells in our mind.
Perhaps even the bile-blood councils can muster
Some chill. Where's the summons?
Court date for reckless tort
Of zero summer, zero spring divine?

Left Hand Cylinder Twist

The university geologist describes
This plate action, skew-tenting fingers over
The hummus and quinoa garden salad.
Then artist bloke expounds his grand theory
That trade wind flow reflects the wash of swells,
Bundled up at shore and inverted over
Arcs of Cascades, Sierra and The Rockies.
His quiet wife, Mekong Delta stock by my
Wretched guess, passes through me with her look,
That same wind through aspens on sawtooth beds,
Her slack gaze out beyond the French speaking
Post-docs and tech pros at the nearby table
From whom I've just excused myself to say
My hellos here among the stocked platters.

I see—I say—it's like a Möbius strip—
And I admit my surprise at the blank stares,
Besides the shy mathematician who grins.
A twist at the coastline—I continue—
Our world's two great outer fluids counter-
Intuitively melded at its only-
Sided surface which at the phoniest scale
Of aberration is the great matter
Our species is found compelled to explore.

A sudden interruption from our host:
Our french confrère *cum* wild west nativist,
Shotgun angled in the air to lick off
Three of the loudest for Bastille to-Day.
Soon came the cross neighbors as expected,
Gesticulating from on-high humorless—
Chief Left Hand's cursive note invites us

To this prime saddle point but offers up
No map for our adventure's onward ride.

. . . As I'd moved on, now engaged with new friends'
Hebrew surname's priestly significance,
While airborne shot imagined screwing through
The cloudy depths would only now be landing,
Splashed down before wading feet of the next
Breaking wave of immigrants to run ramp
Off continental shelf, Chinook leaping
Among fellow journeyers newly and not
So newly arrived. The fortunate ones,
Like Bonny Bight born me landing right here,
Littoral level-up of the billion-
Year bygone sea, become the xeriscaped
Verge on garden of Id in living, eager
Convergence where we make potluck of what
Charms we import from the corners
Of our strip-twist, singular dimension.

Unsprung

White shock startles buds;
Blackbirds peck at false promises,
Aimless in their flocks—
Six-pronged milliard invasion
Drift-damps spring's raucous echoes

Transit of Venus, Fiske Planetarium, Boulder Colorado

We're off work early, eyeing up the clouds,
Our children dancing sun-maker magic twist,
Blowing to whip wind to mist-shifting brisk.
Science and history are the idle chatter here:
From Cook's transit sketches to what future
Space colony might carry Boulder's gist
By the next match for this event on Earth.
The soul of Boulder funnels to the Fiske.

Queues around the amateur telescopes
Bursting into buzz about 4:05
When Venus first pin-punches through the sun disk;
Kids climb, eclipse shades pinned to eyes, the steep
Stone siding, supposing a closer look,
Ushered down by docents mindful of risk;
Odd carnival on the red rock commons—
The soul of Boulder funnels to the Fiske.

The crowd for eclipse just a fortnight ago
Set a world record for such a viewing;
Troll comments on the news went: "Oh Tsk! Tsk!
10,000 folks with nothing better to do?"
But if you've known the Flatiron influence,
The constant stroke of sun, and our obelisk
Of raised, massed hands reaching back up toward, toward…
The soul of Boulder funnels to the Fiske.

Tele Flame

What of these wisp-worn worry lines of mine?
No more than creases on a neat, linen shirt,
Unworthy of their subcutaneous name
Set against those canyons, the hoe-dug woe
On brows of homeowners arranged roadside,
Questioned by reporters: "Oh what a shame!"
Who can feel at helicopter height
The heat behind tinned-up, televised flame.

That's a hawk's sweep from where I lived up north
While down south what thirsty *brenn-baum* monster
Jumped the mountain pass to press the game;
Those houses, ghastly landings for the bouncing
Fire front are larger than mine but placed
For familiar profit, our Front-Range fame;
Yet somehow still abstract, that catastrophe,
Barely half-lit by tinned-up, televised flame.

The flight of these intruders drone, rasping
My roof from Jeffco port, slurry bombers
Ceaseless while the fires burn untamed;
I'm devastated by the need to ask
You to repeat those horrid, drowned-out words,
To double-take a grief my mind can't frame.
Can you across these leagues guide my snookered hand
To some true scorching through this phoned-up flame?

Rare Day

It was my bright-eyed boy pointed out
The stark, stacked, sandstone blocks of NCAR
Flattened against the thrust-up titan slabs,
Brute crown above the muted fields and town;
My own eye was drawn to their bisection
By ash-brushed, flat-bottomed barrier of cloud
Which imposed over our nearest future
Its damp assay, its rainy day reckoning.

Sunshine still served up customary
Hospitality, clearly non-sempiternally
Cooling beneath the peaked cumulus cap,
Highlighting its own retreat, bent back
From early trot of oversized raindrops.

I, day-dreaming the leonine color
Of wildfire along the Poudre northwest,
The Hewlett harassing the gristled green
Around Greyrock, my former hiking grounds.
The wildfire had grown all week beyond hope
Of containment without the weather's help.

It's overwrought to join the starred tokens
Of this gratefully anticipated
Wet front unto Herakles engaged in
Muscle-bound relief, the least complex
In character of superman labors,
But that's what it does to you, this landscape
That struts its favor even against
Parnassos and Olympos, that lures me
To unreasonable covetousness
Of its storied bounties, this obvious haunt

Of the myth-sized, rock-fired fantastical.
Or is that just my gaze, imported poet's?
My boy with his bright eye at myth-hound age
Lights first upon the box of exhibits,
The petting-zoo displays of atmosphere
And space, the gadgetry that tells utter
Tales of solar wind out to heliopause,
Bow shock and Van Allen radiation belts.

It's already old hat, these mist-moistened
Mountains, the fresh, tumbling swell of Poudre,
Of St. Vrain after rain such as today's.
My children, born of this land already
Leap from the world's rooftop to weirding fire
Of blue jets, sprites, aurorae and beyond.
They mind effects of real or imagined
Space weather on their playtime devices.
I see myself as grounding of those circuits,
Providing home perspective for their flights,
Set to vault unmeasured kilometers.
My generation having pushed to the edge
The ecosystems we fancy ourselves
Fit to steward, the young next must relieve
The earth of some portion of our burdens,
Begin to put out the fire of their numbers.

For today, the word is: "Look son! Do look!
The red-grey-green Flatirons and that spreading
Bundle at their crown! A rain day for your
Soccer season finals, and afterward,
Over hot chocolate, I've a few legends,
Tales suitable for just such a rare day."

Autumn Equinox Creature Song

Summer is receding out
Shape up to yell "Shoo!"
The leavings of trees whip through the breeze
And garnish the crumbs we strew;
Away rats: "Shoo!"

Raccoon rattles our dumpster lid,
Coyote prowls the avenue,
Black bear breaks wind from the turkey we binned;
Blaze the spotlight: "Shoo!"

"A mountain lion!" shrills dusk rumor
From the spooked school janitor crew
While timber wolf ghosts and bison by hosts
Stampede our dreamy "Shoo!"

Can't shoot up bobcat shadows:
Ordinance rules out the .22;
However accursed they were here first—
Famous last words: "Shoo!"

Catamount

Que tiene amigo? Léon! Hermoso es!
We all know that poem, that plaint for frost-face,
Done in by poachers mad for yellow pelt;
We teach it to our children in our schools,
Spread wide along the Front Range
And flung in pockets of the moneyed belt
Where diamond mountain life buzzes against
Gold flecks exposed as elder snows melt.

We all think we know her, Colorado queen;
Our kids also taught to fight back if attacked;
Since we spilled into these hills to mine, to smelt,
To ranch, to ogle Sangre de Christo,
to hide away in shacks, to ski Taos
And Steamboat, our settled broods have drip-dealt
Water torture blows against the natives,
Gold flecks exposed as elder snows melt.

Which pity do we choose? Which of us would
Count our child among the million or two
To be clipped and culled? Who here hasn't felt
Stiletto eyes stealthy on their hiking
Family, hailed the wanton trooper's shot?
I have, and yet do cherish those who've long dwelt
Where mankind must now mind land and atmosphere:
Gold flecks exposed as elder snows melt.

Above Left Hand Canyon

For the South Arapaho Legend

I, buffalo-brown transplant, enticed hence
By what Cheyenne would call the pale-suited guide,
Squint past bark beetles engaged in arborcide,
Past insulted, host lodgepole whose shoots heighten
The kite-eye perspective, the skied sense
From green to pale green, from blue to pale blue,
And ash and ash we've smudged where they meet from this view;
These wrongs done Left Hand are past due the righting.

My sightline down this canyon frames two masteries
We residents must reconcile, one of the future,
Heaped with bluff productivity and culture
But sun-blocked by this waste of purchased items,

One age old, O Niwot, before the factories
And territory claims lodged beyond the pale;
Our sly-cinched tenure on this place trembles, frail,
While wrongs done Left Hand are past due the righting.

About the Author

Uche Ogbuji, born in Calabar, Nigeria, had lived, among other places, in Egypt and England, but never anywhere longer than 3 years in his life until he came to Colorado. Here he was instantly smitten by the mountain landscape and cultural flavor and has now settled near Boulder with his wife and four children. Educated mostly in Nigeria, Uche is a computer engineer and entrepreneur whose abiding passion is poetry. His poems, fusing Igbo culture, European Classicism, U.S. Mountain West setting, and Hip-Hop influences, have appeared widely in journals and anthologies. He is editor at Kin Poetry Journal and The Nervous breakdown, founder and curator at the @ColoradoPoetry Twitter project. Uche also snowboards, coaches and plays soccer, and trains in American Kenpo Karate.